Preparing To Die

The Last, Most Important Thing You Will Ever Do

by
Troy L. Gafford

A *Private Label Press* Publication

Double-Edged Publishing
9618 Misty Brook Cove
Cordova, Tennessee 38016

www.doubleedgedpublishing.com

Copyright © 2006 by Double-Edged Publishing, Inc. All rights reserved. No portion of this book may be reproduced—mechanically, electronically, or by any other means, including photocopying—without written permission from the publisher.

ISBN: 978-1-84728-114-2

Double-Edged Publishing, Inc.
9618 Misty Brook Cove
Cordova, Tennessee 38016

www.doubleedgedpublishing.com

Printed in the United States of America
First Printing

Contents

Introduction *1*

Section One—Preparing To Die

Dying Easy 9

Getting Prepared 19

Telling Your Story 55

Saying Good-bye 69

Section Two—Helping ____ Die

Helping To Put Things In Order 83

Giving Voice To Their Story 95

Dealing With Hard Decisions 101

Appendix 117
    Glossary
    Long-Term Care Questions

Dedication

I would like to dedicate this book to my wife Lee Anne. Thanks for the 35-year stroll. One down and one to go.

There's a big old goofy man dancing with a big old goofy girl,

Oh baby, it's a big old goofy world.

John Prine

Acknowledgments

I would like to acknowledge the hard work of many people who made this book possible. For their guidance and technical advice I would like to thank April Holland (and first for being a great daughter), Sunny Ross, Susan Snodgrass, Kittylu Wilbanks, and Becky Wilson. Dennis Willis contributed some special thoughts on the "Going Somewhere" essay and I appreciate his willingness to share those with me. I especially would like my former teacher and current colleague Susan "Boon" Murray for her special insights, and most importantly for instilling the desire in me to see the world through creative eyes, and to look for other explanations than the obvious one.

Mostly my thanks go to Bill Snodgrass, without whom this book could not have been completed. His encouragement was essential.

Introduction

Perhaps there should be a parenthesis attached to the title saying, "or won't do," because in my experience most people put off any discussion of dying, much less preparing to die. It remains one of the last taboo subjects. Most people will talk about money, or even sex, before they will dying. I think this is true of most people, but it seems especially true of "Baby Boomers," the generation of which I am a member. I recently saw an article pointing to the fact that even AARP, the American Association of Retired Persons, decided to change their recruitment pitch to my generation because we seem so resistant to entertaining the thought of joining their organization, because it somehow means acknowledging that we are "over the hill." Part of their strategy was to consider not sending material to anyone just turning 50, and waiting until they turn 55 or 60 might have better results. By that time perhaps the benefits of association might be able to overcome the resistance to considering their own mortality.

Introduction

This reluctance to discuss dying is one of the things I considered when deciding how to structure this book. In reality, my target audience should be anyone with whom God has not shared their departure date for leaving this world. But part of my experience in dealing with the reluctance of people my own age to discuss their own death is that they do have the reality of dealing with the approaching death of their own parents. Thus some of this material, *Section Two*, will be given from the viewpoint of helping someone prepare to die, while the primary section, *Section One*, will be addressed directly to those preparing for themselves. There are additional resources available at my website < www.dyingeasy.net >.

One last word on how the book is structured. I believe that one of the best ways you can help a person complete this last stage of life is to help them recall and tell their life story. This is always one of the topics I stress in any of my seminars. Tell your story. It's one of the best ways to make sense of your life. To encourage people to begin telling their own story, I have added a short story at the end of each chapter dealing with the predominant theme

Introduction

of that section. A short description of my writing style and explanation of the title, *"It's All In How You Study It,"* is included at the end of this section.

Now for the caveats. In this book, I try to offer advice in its basic form, usually in language that everyone can understand. It comes from my experience and from people I come in contact with. I do not have a legal background, so any time I talk about a process that may sound legal it is not to be considered the ultimate word on the subject. People who read this book should contact an attorney any time they have a legal question as processes vary from state to state. For instance, I live in a tri-state area, Arkansas, Mississippi, and Tennessee, and laws and procedures may vary from state to state. Therefore, first take any advice for what it is, advice, and be sure to contact a legal source any time you are dealing with legal matters. Second, I will not attempt to talk about every issue dealing with death. There are too many, and when people have more expertise than I do in a particular subject, I will refer you to their publications or websites.

Introduction

It's All In How You Study It...

Much of my writing style comes from hearing my grandparents, uncles, aunts, and other relatives talk as I was a child, grownup talk when they thought I wasn't listening. I still remember many of their sayings, but more importantly, the wisdom behind them. And while today as I remember them they bring back pleasant memories, my grandparents gave them to me as life lessons. Some were things I should do to bring good luck, or more importantly, things I should not do to avoid bad luck. I learned how to wish on a star, count buzzards, stamp gray mules, peel an apple, what a pulley bone was good for, and the right way to hang a horseshoe over a door. And I knew what things to avoid, don't handle frogs, be careful about looking at a grasshopper too closely, and if a turtle bit you he would hold on to you until it thundered. I learned that unless you wanted it to rain you should never hang a dead snake belly side up on a barbed wire fence or sun a feather mattress. I also learned things you could do to deal with bad luck

Introduction

omens, from black cats, a rabbit running across the road in front of an automobile, and what to do if a cow is about to cross the road in front of you. I knew better than to ask if I could go fishing on Sunday, and I never saw my grandmother sew on Sunday. If it was not a sin, it was, at least, very bad luck. In her house you didn't twirl a chair around on one leg, sing at the supper table, open umbrellas, throw a hat on a bed, or put shoes underneath one.

Well now to the title. Sometimes when I would ask my grandparents or other relatives a question, the answer would be, "It's all in how you study it." Today people would say, "It depends." Some things were not up for debate, and in those situations the answers were clear, either yes or no. But in some circumstances, it was a shade of gray, not a clear black or white answer. Later on in life, it helped to explain how people could have completely different versions of the same event. More than once I heard my grandmother say, "No matter how flat you make a pancake, it's flat on both sides." There are at least two sides to every story. That way of looking at things has stuck with me throughout my life. I try to look at things

Introduction

from different angles and find other explanations for a person's behavior other than the one I initially attribute it to. I try not to assign blame because blame involves intent, and sometimes a person's behavior is not as much sinister as it is simply stupid. And this is how I began to write down my thoughts and how I dealt with certain situations. Sometimes it would turn into a story, but more often than not it would just help me make sense of what I was going through. Hopefully these stories will help add some texture to the topics discussed in each chapter and will encourage you to begin telling your own story.

Preparing To Die

CHAPTER ONE

Dying Easy

The fear of dying is almost assuredly universal and probably increases for most people as they get older. But what are some factors that contribute to this fear? The fear of the process may actually be worse than the product when it comes to dying. One reason for fear is that it is so hard to get anyone to talk about death, at least directly. It's hard for many people to even say the words death and dying. Often they are referred to as having, "passed on" or, "gone to a better place." But if they do discuss death, and if you ask them how they want to die, most people say the perfect scenario would be to die one night in their sleep - just go to sleep and, painlessly during the night, it's over. And, oh by the way, can you let me know about five years ahead of time so I can get ready? But as I watch people die, I notice that some people seem to die easier than others.

By dying easy, I mean they have a sense of ease about dying. They have worked through the process. They have the philosophy that life has been good to them overall and seem to be prepared to die. Others seem to die hard, and I don't necessarily mean physically. There is a sense of anger, denial, and sometimes bitterness. Life has not necessarily been good to them, and they may even die alone with little family or social support. The more I think about it, being prepared seems to be a big part of it. Denying that it will happen, or putting off dealing with important issues, only seems to make the process harder. It's like my grandmother used to say, "One road is as good as another if you don't know where you're going."

Being prepared sounds like they had a job to do and they did it. And I'm not sure that characterization is far from the truth. While in college, I became familiar with life stage development theory. Life stage development theory is much more than life has a beginning and an end.

In layman's terms, it is based on a developmental theory that each stage of life has its own requirements for completion, and if a person does not complete one stage they will have difficulty completing later stages. For instance, you are going to find it difficult to learn higher forms of math if you didn't master the basics of addition and subtraction. In real life, a young girl who has a baby at 15, before she graduates from high school, may experience difficulty in completing later life stages unless considerable resources are provided, such as child care, so that she can complete high school or at least get her GED. I am not choosing to discuss in depth the theory of life stage development, but if anyone wants to explore that topic further, they should consult Erik Erickson (Erickson, 1950) and Daniel Levinson (Levinson, D.J. & et. al., 1978).

Simply put, throughout life you have stages to go through and jobs to accomplish. When you are young, your role is to be a student and your job is to go to school. After you marry, your job is to become a parent and assume those responsibilities. And throughout your life you assume many roles. Many of the problems people have in their lives relate to how they have successfully completed a life stage, and how these stages build upon each other. Failure to successfully complete a life stage is often a recipe for disaster.

This is one of the difficulties in dealing with death, and why most people would be better served to begin to deal with this process, even now. No one knows when it's going to happen, so often they aren't prepared if the end comes at them suddenly. They know it's out there, but most people think it's way out there. But what if it's not way out there, but right around the corner? We see people die at literally every age, and often remark how unfair it is. And, it is, often cruelly unfair. But, wouldn't it be better to be prepared? I believe that the dying process is just another life stage you have to complete. Well maybe not just another life stage, because I believe it is a very important life stage, as you can tell by the title of this book. Part of my ministry is to help people successfully prepare to complete this life stage. More specifically, I believe you can either die hard or you can die easy. And in hard or easy, I'm not talking about physical issues, but more social, emotional, and spiritual issues.

Earlier I talked about wanting to know ahead of time when you were going to die, and how nice that would be. Sometimes that is the case, and I was one of the lucky ones. About eight years ago I received a terminal diagnosis from the doctor and have been going through my own personal process of discovery ever since. And I'm lucky, because I asked for five years to get ready and received it. And do you know one of the things I found out? If you prepare like you're going to die in five years, and you live past that time, you feel like you're way ahead of the game. It's all gravy. And as I began to prepare for death, I found out that for me being prepared made things easier. And in life stage development theory, knowing what the requirements are for a particular life stage, and the resources you have available to you, can help maximize positive outcomes and minimize negative ones. I believe the same is true in preparing to die. At least it was for me. Therefore I encourage you to think about beginning this process for yourself. This is one of the purposes of this book, to provide you with the resources to do this.

Erikson, E. (1950). *Childhood and Society*. New York: Horton.

Levinson, D.J., Darrow, C.N., Klein, E.B., Levinson, M.H., & McKee, B. (1978). *The Seasons of a Man's Life*. New York: Knopf, Inc.

It's All In How You Study It...

Whistling Past The Graveyard

Most people consider me a little unusual when it comes to funerals. Like a lot of people, I don't like them, and I always tell people not to take it personally if I don't attend their funeral. I tell them that I just don't do funerals. I have been to a few of my direct family members, but over the years I can count the number of funerals I've attended on one hand. I still might go for visitation and pay my respects, but seldom do I attend the actual funeral.

But as much as I dislike funerals, I love cemeteries. This is especially true for older cemeteries. There's so much history there, and oh the stories you can hear, if you can just fine-tune your hearing. You can look around at the headstones and just hear their unusual stories. I visited one historic cemetery and wondered how devastated a mother must have been when she had three children die on three consecutive days. Not only did she have to deal with three deaths so close to each other, they were her children and your children are not supposed to die ahead of you. If you lose a spouse, you're a widow or widower, and if you lose your parents, you're an orphan. But there's no label when you lose your children, perhaps because it's a concept that's so foreign to the rhythmic cycle of life that society hasn't been able to apply a name to it. And just how long do you think it took for that hole in her heart to heal? It may have not completely been able to heal until her own death eight years later.

I've seen husband and wife die within days of each other and wonder if it was because of injuries from a shared accident or if the remaining spouse just couldn't heal their broken heart after the other one died. Sometimes there are a number of years between their deaths, but you wonder about the quality of those remaining years, especially if most of that time was spent grieving their loss. I've visited other cemeteries where veterans are buried who have given their lives in wars dating back to the Civil War and wondered if I had been born in that time, would I have suffered a similar fate? Each grave represents a life, and all that life represented.

As I was visiting the cemetery where my daughters are buried the other day, I looked around at some of the graves as I often do and was reminded that change takes place even here. Gone are the traditional headstones that used to mark graves in most older cemeteries. In their place are flat markers that are easier for the grounds crew to maintain. But as I was looking around I noticed that the new markers no longer use one of the most important symbols found on the older styles.

Most of us are familiar with the style that lists the date of birth with a dash or hyphen followed by the date of death, and it's that dash or hyphen that got me to thinking one day. I call it a dash even though on a headstone that symbol may have its own name. Even if it doesn't, then maybe it should, because it represents a great deal if you think about it. It's more than a separator of the days they were born or died. It's the life in between. That dash

Dying Easy

represents that person's entire life. For some that dash represents few events because their life was short, maybe only days, but for the average person it represents an almost limitless number of points that correspond to an equal number of life experiences. It would be great to be able to see that life under a microscope and be able to draw out a specific slice and see how that event shaped their character or defined their existence.

In our Southern culture we don't always deal well with death, but it's always there. Sometimes it's a tragedy, and sometimes it's simply a mystery, part of a natural rhythm or not.

CHAPTER TWO

Getting Prepared

As I mentioned earlier, as I began to prepare for death, I found out that for me being prepared made things easier. Easier, but still not easy. Even if you have some time to prepare for your death, it still doesn't make it easy. The first areas I concentrated on were financial matters. I had worked hard for many years to make a life for me and my family, so I wanted to protect my assets, my money, property, etc., as much as I could. I began to think about documents such as a will, different kinds of advance directives, probate, trusts, long-term care, and other financial and legal matters.

Getting Prepared

WILL

You would be surprised by how many people die *intestate*, or without a written will. It still happens every day. Well, it does, and it doesn't. You can die without having left any written instructions on how you want your material possessions distributed, but you really can't die without a will. If you die without a will, the state will provide you with one, and the manner in which your possessions will be distributed is written in the law. Most people who die without a written will want the proceeds of their estate to flow directly to their survivors, and they simply don't get around to writing a will. You may have told your children that you want them to have certain items of yours after you've died, but you have no guarantee of that occurring unless it's written down. This happens often when dealing with second spouses and children, or where there has been a bitter divorce in the past that was never reconciled. The best advice is to make your wishes known to as many people as possible, but also to write those wishes down. Many people leave the question of what will happen to their assets to the courts. But by completing at a

Getting Prepared

minimum a will, and more importantly an estate plan, you will have legal documents that specify how your assets will be handled after your death. One of the things that I hope this book accomplishes is to increase the dialogue among people so that their wishes are completely known to everyone, but especially among family members.

ADVANCE DIRECTIVES

When you mention the term advance directives to most people, they automatically think about end-of-life documents in the event you become unable to speak for yourself. The two most popular are the *living will* and the *health care power of attorney*. These instructions are usually spelled out in a prepared document, but they can also be oral in some states. Each state is responsible for determining the use of advance directive documents, and how they are regulated differs from state to state. Some states offer pre-approved living will documents, so check with your individual state agency if you have any questions. One pre-approved document that is accepted in

Getting Prepared

many states is called *Five Wishes*. It is a very simple document that is laid out in worksheets that are very easy to understand and complete. You can find out more about *Five Wishes* at 1-888-5WISHES or at their website < www.agingwithdignity.org >. Additionally many hospitals and agencies dealing with aging populations have these forms.

Most of the discussion of advance directives will center on the *living will* and the *health care power of attorney*, but in this section we will also consider how to make your financial wishes known as well, so we will discuss *wills*, *living trusts*, *probate*, and *power of attorney*. This discussion will be at a layman's level and you should always consult an attorney familiar with elder issues to formulate your own plan for dealing with any long-term care issues. I certainly am not a lawyer, and make no claims to expertise in any legal area. Discussion of these topics is meant to encourage you to plan ahead for your long-term care plan. This will make planning for your ultimate death easier, which is always the aim of this book and the website.

Getting Prepared

LIVING WILL & HEALTH CARE POWER OF ATTORNEY

A *living will* is a legal document that says you don't wish to be hooked up to any life support systems that artificially prolong life in the event you are terminally ill or permanently unconscious and unable to communicate. A *health care power of attorney* (in some states referred to as a durable power of attorney for health care), authorizes someone to act on your behalf as your attorney-in-fact in making your medical decisions, after it has been determined that you can no longer act in this capacity. Your health care power of attorney does not have to be a lawyer. In fact, most of the time, it is someone very close to you who you trust to carry out your previously expressed decisions.

Some people have both of these documents because each one offers something that the other does not. The living will remains in effect even if your health care power of attorney is unable to perform their duties. It acts as reinforcement in case someone challenges their decisions, and can even provide assurance that they are in fact following your wishes. Having this agent also protects you in case a scenario comes up that you might not have anticipated. It ensures that someone you trust, and who has knowledge of your general wishes and nature, has the decision-making ability to make those unanticipated decisions that might arise. You maintain as much control over your health care as possible because you've planned ahead, and someone you trust has your decision-making ability just in case.

A living will basically states that you don't want to have your life prolonged by artificial means after a doctor has determined that you are terminally ill and have no chance of recovery. State law has given you the right to accept or refuse such treatment. In most states it can be handwritten, but usually it is drawn up by an attorney or by using a preprinted form. It must be witnessed by two people who do not have an interest in your death, and they can't be relatives, heirs, or health care providers. Discussing these topics with your relatives and your

Getting Prepared

physician is essential. These decisions are very personal and are a reflection of your beliefs and values. The real key is to plan ahead and make these decisions before someone else makes them for you when you no longer can.

One of the drawbacks of a living will is that it only becomes pertinent when a doctor has determined that you're not going to live. However a health care power of attorney can authorize medical treatment decisions before things get to this point. You have authorized them to speak for you anytime you are unable to do so for yourself, not just when someone has decided that you are terminally ill. It's about maintaining control and quality of life issues, not just being alive, and focuses on what's important to you, your attitudes of: independence and control, death and dying, and religious beliefs.

Advance directives don't become relevant as long as you can make your own decisions, but if you are in an accident or become seriously ill, you know that someone you trust will make those decisions for you. Your health care power of attorney has the power to make all decisions

Getting Prepared

regarding your health care, including health care providers, medical treatment, and life support decisions, as well as donating your organs for research or how your body will be disposed of unless you have written your document to restrict them in these decisions. You also have the right to revoke the health care power of attorney, in writing, at any time before you become incapacitated.

Advance directives are important for you because they insure that your wishes for your medical care are respected, but they can also be valuable for your caregiver. They reinforce your wishes when it comes time to make the difficult decisions. These decisions are personal in nature and should reflect your beliefs and attitudes while respecting your wishes. After you have completed these documents, you should put the original in a secure place. Make copies and give to your agent, your physician, and anyone else who might be involved with your health care.

You may have already named someone in your will to act as your power of attorney in the event you become incapacitated, sometimes referred to as a springing power

Getting Prepared

of attorney, but you may also want to have a health care power of attorney because of the specific nature of making medical decisions. In fact, these can be two different people. It also protects you in case the state passes a law in the future that restricts what a living will can and can't do.

PROBATE

There are actually two types of *probate*, *death probate* and *disability probate*. Most people only associate the term probate to the process associated with your death, but there can be a probate process associated with your disability. If you become disabled, everything in your sole name can be at risk for the probate process. If you have appointed a durable power of attorney in your will that springs into effect upon your disability, you may be protected, but most people have not done this. Even then, there are some instances when this does not keep the process from happening. In the disability probate process, you will have to hire an attorney, there may have to be a

Getting Prepared

conservator appointed, and there is the possibility of litigation, especially in the case of blended families.

The probate process most people are familiar with is the death probate. At a person's death, any assets in their sole name are frozen and are subject to the probate process, even if there is a will. If you don't have a will, the state will give you one. There are prescribed rules on how a person's estate is to be divided if there is no valid will, and it might not be the way you would have wanted it to be divided. So make sure you have a will. One of the reasons for probate is so that any creditors can file a claim with the person's estate, and the state and federal government are the first in line. The negative aspects most of us associate with probate center around the issues of time, cost, and the fact that the proceedings become part of the public record.

There are certain things that pass through, or avoid, probate. One of these is assets that are in joint name with rights of survivorship, such as real estate or a joint bank account. Another is life insurance. It usually flows right to the designated beneficiary. But this is one area where it might be advisable to check with a qualified tax professional to see how it affects your estate. Most people consider benefits from a life insurance policy to be tax free, and while it is true that the proceeds are not subject to income tax, that may not be the case with the probate process if it puts you above the exemption level. This is especially true of many couples who purchase term insurance in the one million dollar category. If they were to die at the same time, suddenly their estate has a two million dollar value, and this would be above the exemption level. Some of these issues are too complicated to discuss here, and this is the area where a qualified tax professional can assist you in the area of estate planning and living trusts. This will be discussed more fully in a separate section. A proper estate plan will seek to take advantage of existing laws to save every possible dollar of estate and inheritance tax while making sure you retain control over how your assets pass to whomever you want and in the manner you prescribe.

One of the ways to avoid probate is to create a *revocable living trust*. There is an entire industry devoted to these trusts and you can imagine how many different factors can be associated with them, so I can only discuss them in general terms here. Any discussions concerning trusts are not to be taken as legal advice, so be sure to consult a qualified tax professional. I will only seek to discuss these issues in basic terms with the goal of providing you information that will help you make informed choices in your estate planning.

REVOCABLE LIVING TRUST

There are a number of reasons why you might consider establishing a *revocable living trust*. The primary reason is to maintain control over your estate at your death, or in the event you become disabled. It allows you to leave your assets to whom you want, when you want, how you want, and in the most tax efficient manner. It will also help you to avoid probate. One way to look at a trust is to consider it like starting a company. You create a company, the trust, and everything is owned by the company. It avoids probate because there are no assets left at death.

Getting Prepared

They are distributed in the prescribed manner set forth in the document so there are no assets for the court to probate. It takes your assets out of the jurisdiction of the court. It also gives you greater control over your assets in the case of disability. It avoids having to hire an attorney and a conservator appointed by the court to act as your guardian.

How do you determine if a living trust is for you? As stated above, control is the primary factor. One of the other points to consider is cost. You might not need a trust if the cost of setting up and maintaining the trust is more than the cost of probate. Additionally it depends on how much of the work you are willing to do in maintaining the trust, because anytime you sell or replace an asset it has to be retitled. Many administrators will provide you with the forms necessary to identify all of your assets and get them reassigned to the trust. If you don't want to do the leg work in going to title companies and financial institutions, they will do it for you, but at a charge. You can name yourself or another family member as the trustee. Just remember there should be a regular time, perhaps annually, that you

Getting Prepared

look at your assets and make sure the trust structure is in proper order.

In closing, there are a number of factors to determine if a living trust is for you. The main consideration is control over your assets. Additionally, it saves time and money upon your death by avoiding probate. However a living trust is a legal contract on paper and if properly constructed can be a complicated one that might be better completed by a professional. The people who tell you that you can attend a one-day seminar and create your own living trust might not really have your best interests at heart. They may be only concerned with selling you something. As with anything discussed in this book or the website, consult a qualified professional if you have any questions. A living trust is a higher order of advance directive. Make sure you have the basic advance directives covered first, along with your will and if you desire, a living will or medical power of attorney. These are discussed more fully in another section.

Getting Prepared

LONG-TERM CARE

What is your plan to provide for your long-term care needs? Everyone has one. It may be procrastination, but you may need a better plan. Now is the time to plan how you're going to pay for the expenses you're going to face unless you die very suddenly. You should realize that you, or someone close to you, may face a chronic condition requiring intensive care, either at home or in a nursing home. In fact one of the reasons you may be aware of this situation is that you have helped a loved one go through the dying process and were shocked at the expenses involved and how ill prepared you were. The funds to pay for these expenses are going to come from one or more of the following areas: private savings, investments (such as IRA's), family members, long-term care insurance, or from some form of government assistance. According to the United States Health Care Financing Administration (HCFA), the agency of the federal government that oversees our country's long-term health care industry, about 30% of all long-term care expenses are paid for by individuals or their families out of their own pocket. About

Getting Prepared

40% are paid by Medicaid, though there are a lot of strings attached to receiving this money. This will be covered more fully in another section. The rest are paid for by Medicare or from other sources.

Many people don't take their long-term care plan more seriously because they mistakenly think they will be covered by Medicare, by Medicare supplemental insurance, by their own health insurance, or they just assume that one day the federal government will eventually cover them. According to the U.S. Agency on Aging, the number of elderly over 65 will increase every year for the next 50 years. While it is true that as the "Baby Boomer" generation ages and becomes more politically powerful there may be some type of universal long-term insurance, it does not currently exist. In our local tri-state area, Tennessee, Arkansas, and Mississippi, there is a growing movement to place more emphasis on home and community-based services and away from the nursing home. States are exploring Medicaid waivers through certain trial programs in order to provide more services from a stretched budget, where the cost is lower than

Getting Prepared

nursing home care. So far these are very limited. Also there are no assurances that the budget crisis that many states are experiencing is close to being resolved. While the trend is to provide more care in the home and at adult day care centers, the bottom line is that you just can't depend on the government to provide for your long-term care needs.

Medicare primarily covers doctor fees, medical expenses, and hospital visits. There are a few instances where Medicare pays for long-term care, such as rehabilitation or specialty care after an acute episode, such as breaking a hip. However coverage is very limited and only for short periods of time. Medicare pays only when you have been hospitalized for at least three days. Services have to be prescribed by a physician, and have to be given in a skilled nursing facility approved by Medicare. Even then Medicare will only pay for 90 days.

As mentioned earlier, about 40% of long-term expenses are covered by Medicaid, but basically you have to deplete all of your income and assets to $2,000. There are some provisions for a spouse to keep some money above this level, but you really need to seek the advice of a qualified professional when it comes to these exceptions. Some people will tell you that you just need to purposely spend down your assets, but this takes a lot of planning. You need to be very careful how you do this because it is technically illegal under the Health Insurance Accountability Act of 1996 to shelter your assets in order to qualify for Medicaid. It becomes especially complex when you're dealing with tangible assets, such as your house, because the federal government looks at assets sold under fair market value and can look back at an individual's transactions for five years. There have been instances where states have forced heirs to sell their parent's house after their death to repay Medicaid. You can plan ahead legally through trusts and other legal instruments to protect your estate. This will be covered in more detail in another section, but you need good legal advice and proper planning in advance. Do not use any advice in this book or the website as any basis for a legal opinion.

Growing old is better in most cases than the alternative, so plan now to grow older and start planning for your long-term care needs. Long-term care insurance is one of the planning tools you may want to consider.

LONG-TERM CARE INSURANCE

One of the ways to help finance your long-term care costs is to purchase long-term care (LTC) insurance. It provides money when you need care for activities you can no longer provide for yourself, and for supervised care if you develop dementia. In-home care and adult day care can be covered by it, and assisted-living facilities and nursing homes accept it. One of the primary points to keep in mind is that you need to consider purchasing this insurance when you are healthy, preferably at a younger age when it is more affordable, because if you wait until your health is poor you might not be able to afford it, or even purchase it.

Getting Prepared

Long-term care insurance is becoming more popular with approximately one million policies sold each year, but you have to determine if it is for you. One of the primary reasons to purchase LTC is if you have significant assets and you want to make sure they pass through to your estate. It can protect your assets and prevent what you spent your entire life accumalating from going down the drain, or going to the government if you have to spend down your assets to qualify for Medicaid. It also gives you some control over your situation if you have to go to a nursing home. If you have to depend on Medicaid, you may not be able to live in the nursing home you would choose for yourself, and your quality of life may diminish from what you're accustomed to. It might be wise to consult a good financial planner who specializes in estate planning and elder issues to make sure you retain as much control over your health care issues as possible and guarantee that your estate passes to your heirs as intact as possible.

A good LTC insurance policy will pay for in-home care and adult day care centers as well as in a variety of assisted-living facilities and nursing homes. Make sure

Getting Prepared

your policy pays for homemaker services and any necessary home modifications so you can remain in your home as long as possible, where you are most comfortable. Most policies waive the premium in the event that you need care, but you should make sure that it covers all care, including in-home care, and not just institutional care. Keep in mind however that whenever you purchase more options, such as inflation protection or return of premium, the cost increases. Also you must decide how much coverage you will need. An agent will offer you a daily benefit and you will decide how many years of coverage you wish to purchase. You may have to balance these two questions when you consider a policy. Do you want to concentrate more on an adequate daily benefit or longevity of stay? You always have to remember when you're purchasing a LTC policy you are buying a specific pool of funds. Once the funds are depleted, they are gone. A LTC policy is unique. It is not life insurance and it is not health insurance. It is a hybrid.

Moreover this points to one of the primary concerns in purchasing LTC insurance. In fact, it is such an important issue that there is a 30-day provision to change your mind and receive a full refund. You have to consider at what age you will need the funds and if you will be able to continue paying the premiums until then. If you quit paying premiums, in many cases you will receive nothing. There is a clause in most policies called a non-forfeiture option where you will receive a limited amount of coverage if you discontinue paying premiums, but it is limited and you must pay premiums for four or five years before this clause kicks in. There is no cash value associated with most of these policies, so if you never use the policy, there is no payout. You have just spent the money for peace of mind, unless you purchase options such as return of premium or you purchase a policy that is actually a life insurance product with the payments for long-term care made through an attached rider.

So, how much does it cost? Prices vary from region to region throughout the country. It's certainly cheaper in our local tri-state area, Tennessee, Arkansas, and Mississippi, than it is in the New York, Chicago, or San Francisco area, but on average, a 25-year old may pay as

Getting Prepared

little as $800 per year and a 75-year old may pay over $10,000 per year. You can also choose different payment plans, from annually, 10-year pay, and single premium. One you might want to consider is the 10-year pay, because after that ten year period your premiums are paid in full and can't be raised for many companies. You have to make sure of that in your policy, because some companies can send you an assessment even after you have quit paying premiums. You can also add more bells and whistles, such as inflation protection, but that will increase the premium. Also, your premiums can be raised, but not individually. They can only be raised on the entire class, such as every 55-year old male.

Long-term care insurance can be a valuable tool to help in your long-term care plans, but it is only one piece of the puzzle in your plan and you have to determine where, or if, it fits into your plan. I have added an additional table in the appendix with questions you might want to ask yourself and some terms to understand before you purchase a LTC insurance policy.

Getting Prepared

VETERAN BENEFITS

Benefits are available to veterans for both in-home and assisted living care that many people are not aware of. It was enacted by Congress a little over a decade ago to help keep people in their homes and out of hospitals and nursing homes where expenses are higher. You have to qualify for it and it is basically tied to how much income you earn each month. Your house and car are exempt, but any income from investments such as interest from certificates of deposit and annuities must be declared. You have to declare all your monthly income and subtract your expenses, and then if you qualify you will receive a monthly check to help defray those expenses. One of the benefits of this money is once you receive it you don't have to document what you spend it on. You are free to spend it any way you wish. There is a lag time after you apply for benefits, but if you qualify, the benefits are retroactive to the date of application, similar to social security benefits.

It is available to veterans who served at least 75 active duty days in World War I, World War II, the Korean

Getting Prepared

War, and Vietnam. Additionally, they must be at least 55 years old, and they must have been honorably discharged. On the application be sure to include the rank at discharge and any medals or special citations because these receive priority. It is also available to widows of veterans, subject to certain conditions. Many geriatric care managers and assisted living administrators are familiar with this program and can assist you in filling out the proper forms. Also the Social Work Department of any VA hospital will be able to assist you.

Getting Prepared

It's All In How You Study It...

Brandie

I realize that as I write this, not everyone will relate to it the same way I do. Just as there are dogs that are not really friendly toward people, not everyone is a dog person. Those of you that are, know who you are, and maybe the rest of you will understand the principles involved and still get something from it.

Just how do you deal with losing the best dog in the world, at least the best you've come across? More specifically, how do you grieve the loss when you're grieving the loss of the one who has helped you grieve all your other losses? Brandie came into our lives because of loss. It was July 4th weekend in 1991, when we lost a young puppy due to parvo disease. About two weeks later, my daughter and I went and picked out Brandie, a seven-

Getting Prepared

week old Golden Retriever, and soon thereafter she began the work that she was so good at - helping the healing process begin. Within a short while, we began to get over the loss of the first puppy. Even though it was not easy, it was easier because of her, and she would do it over and over again during her twelve years with us.

She was perfect for our family, my wife and I, our oldest daughter, and our set of special needs twin girls. The twins had severe disabilities and were thirteen years old when we got Brandie, and they loved her. Even as a puppy she was well behaved and was perfect for the girls. They lit up when she came around and especially enjoyed seeing me get on the floor and roll around with her. I can still hear their laughter. Probably even more amazing, she seemed to develop a sense of when they were about to go through one of their seizures and tried to tell us about it. I have since heard about this from other people and stories I've read, but it's always been real to me. She always seemed to be on their wave length, even though they were never able to communicate verbally.

She loved being around people, and though she was certainly friendly around other dogs, she really preferred human companionship. That's one of the traits that made her such a great dog for me. She always had me or my wife, or someone helping with the twins, around her 24 hours a day her entire life. There were probably not more than 60 days in the last ten years that either my wife or myself were away from her. Not only did she provide therapy for me, she was a therapy dog in reality. For over a year she accompanied me to two hospital units where she gave that unconditional love and acceptance that she was so good at. But I had to quit taking her after she was diagnosed with hip problems at age four. I could tell she really missed it, but I knew it was better for her. After that I had to make sure that I spent even more special time with her to make up for what she was missing. But as good as she was as a therapy dog at the hospital, her real gift was in providing therapy to me as I needed it over the next few years.

The first occasion was after one of the twins died in 1995, just before her 18th birthday. Our daughter had

Getting Prepared

experienced a lot of pain in her last few years, and even though I was glad she was in Heaven and in pain no longer, I really missed her and her sweet smile. Brandie helped me through that time so well and over the next eight years she would do it again and again. I am convinced it was not just fate that brought Brandie to us. An actual angel from Heaven couldn't have provided any more of what we needed. Four years later she would be there once again when on Father's Day in 1999 the other twin would finally go to be with her sister.

Just a few months earlier I had been diagnosed with lymphoma and this is the area where she really did her best therapy. Until she died four years later, she was my constant companion and counselor. Her greatest joy was just being around me and doing whatever I was doing. She was the perfect dog to work in the yard with. She loved being outside and doing whatever I wanted to do. If it was time to cut the yard, she loved to watch. In fact, she had a regular routine. After I would cut the back yard, she would go to the same spot every time up on the hill and lie down and watch me finish the front yard or the edging. From this

Getting Prepared

vantage point, she could see everything that was going on and enjoyed lying in the freshly mown grass, especially rolling around trying to scratch her back.

She was not the type of dog that I ever had to worry about running away, and believe me I've had the ones that you couldn't let out the front door unless they were on a leash. And if they got past you when the front door was open, they were gone like a flash and they weren't coming back just because you called them. She did like to go on walks, only with one of us. In fact, the people in the neighborhood were always amazed when we would walk, because she had the most unusual habit. Once you picked up the leash, she became excited and once walking she would always want to take the leash from you and walk down the sidewalk with the leash in her mouth, walking herself. This was especially funny when we went to the vet. She would willingly walk into the office but once we had been there a few minutes, she would come and take the leash in her mouth and walk over to the door, telling us she wanted to go. Everyone in the office would always get a kick out of her behavior.

Getting Prepared

And as we both got older and my energy level began to decrease even more, she even became my barometer to monitor how hard I worked. As we both became more easily fatigued, she enjoyed the more frequent breaks we had to take. She would go with me to set under the fans, and after a rest we would be at it again. The only thing she couldn't stand was being inside when I was outside. She would stand at the back door and bark until she got your attention, and this was about the only time she would bark. I'll never forget the first time I heard her bark. She was about three years old, and I had never heard her bark before, and even then it was to let me know she wanted to be where I was. She seldom barked for any other reason. She didn't bark at other dogs or become the nuisance dog that many people have for neighbors—the one that seems to bark whenever a leaf falls and continues barking for what seems forever.

Two years ago she was also diagnosed with cancer. When I took her to the vet and had the growth removed, we had even more in common. As I helped her during her

Getting Prepared

recovery process from surgery, I began to realize even more what she had done for me. I would sometimes even think about who would live longer. Well, while my condition began to stabilize, her cancer did come back a few weeks ago as the vet said it might. This time it seemed to settle in her hips, which had already deteriorated, and in the last few days made it almost impossible to walk. I knew it was finally time to think about easing her pain three days before her death. I was going outside to mow the yard and she didn't want to come. Now she had almost quit wanting to go on our daily walks, and we hadn't taken one in a few days because I could tell the pain was becoming too much. She would hardly go a few yards and sit down waiting for me to come back for her, and we would go back in. We even had to start going in and out a side door because there were no steps involved. She couldn't even make the two steps through our normal door because of the stress it put on her hips. But it was especially troubling to me when she didn't want to go outside with me to mow the yard. This was one of her favorite activities, and even the sound of the lawnmower couldn't get her to the door. I finished mowing the back

Getting Prepared

yard and went into the room and saw her straining to get up and unable to do so. I went back outside and put the lawnmower up and came back to the room, and I just stretched down on the floor next to her and we spent the next hour just loving each other.

Two nights later was July 4th and as usual one of her least favorite times because of the loud fireworks. We went to bed early that night because we were all tired and emotionally spent, and near midnight I was awakened by an extremely loud blast and could hear her down at the foot of the bed. I could tell she was upset and wanted to get over closer to where I slept but couldn't get up, so I laid down with her and stroked her and told her how much I loved her until she had calmed down and went back to sleep.

The next day, my wife and I knew it was time to go to the vet and ease her suffering, and as we made that drive, she reminded me of how things had come full circle. It was July 4th weekend twelve years ago that through our grief we began the process of inviting a special dog into our lives, an event that would impact our lives forever. And I say

Getting Prepared

forever because I believe, as most true dog people will tell you, I will see her again one day. Even now I can see her running and playing with the twins.

When we arrived at the vet, there was someone at the side door to help us because we didn't want to go through the front waiting area and upset the other people as they saw us carrying a dog and crying; and believe me the tears were uncontrollable. When we got her onto the examination table, things went quickly; in fact, quicker than I thought they would. The vet agreed with us that we were doing the right thing and helped us through the process because she could see how hard it was on us. She told my wife and I to get up next to her head so that the last thing she would see were the people who loved her the most. As we were talking to her, the vet found the vein and gave her the shot. She was resting on her front paws so she could hold her head next to us and we were just telling her how much we loved her and kissing her on the side of her face like she always liked. Within seconds, she eased back down on her side and the vet moved to her side, checked for a heartbeat, and told us she was gone. We then kissed

Getting Prepared

her one last time, told her we loved her, and made our way through the tears to the car and back home.

When I arrived back home, it was looking like it was going to rain, but I thought there was enough time to finish mowing the yard that I had started three days earlier. It would also give me something to do. I know the neighbors might have thought I was crazy, but fortunately you can't really tell someone is crying as they mow the yard from that far across the street. About every couple of trips I would either look up to the spot where she normally would be or hear what sounded like her barking from inside the house, but eventually I finished before the rain came. In fact, it reminded me of one of my favorite memories of the times we enjoyed. I have always enjoyed the time right before a good stormy rain. She never really liked thunder or any loud noises, but often she would come with me to the swing on the back porch. There I could enjoy the wind and the smell that often comes before a good rain, but still be close enough to come in before the rain started. So I put up the mower and walked around to the swing. Through the tears that would flow often over the next few days, I

Getting Prepared

saw in my mind's eye many of the times we enjoyed and told her how much I loved her and appreciated what she had done for me. Within a few minutes the raindrops began to fall, and we quickly went back into the house because she never liked the rain. Let the healing begin again.

CHAPTER THREE

Telling Your Story

My friend Boon likes to quote Anatole Broyard, a New York Times book critic, who said "people bleed stories." That is especially true as we get older. It becomes important that we are known for who we are, all that we are, both the good and the bad. One of the ways we can do this is to recount our stories, especially the ones we hold on to, the ones that define us. In addition, sometimes our stories help us deal with loss in our life. I believe a person's history of how they deal with loss can be a predictor of how they approach their own mortality. Much of life has to do with loss, or at least how you deal with it. As you get older, things get taken from you, but often you don't realize this until after they're gone. Then what do

Telling Your Story

you do? People who are not successful in dealing with loss don't necessarily suffer more losses than people who are able to deal with loss effectively. One of the things that helped me to deal with loss was to get to the point where I made a choice. I was either going to continue to grieve for what I lost, or didn't have, or focus on what I still had. There is no set time limit for grieving. It may be short or long, and it is not tied to how much you loved and who, what, or how much you lost. I began long ago writing down my thoughts about my life experiences and found that writing helped me deal with them. Now my thoughts don't always turn onto a story, but they always help me make sense of the process.

For many people I come in contact with there is an initial resistance to telling their life story. For some, it centers around the fact that they don't believe they can write very well. They begin right away telling me that English was their worst subject in school and they were just never any good at writing. For others it is all the negative self-talk. *Nobody is interested in my story. I'm just not that interesting.* Or, *I've lived an interesting life, but there are*

Telling Your Story

just not many things in it I'm proud of. I always tell them that's not the important thing. Don't approach this from the daunting task of having to write the great American novel. Just start slowly. If you feel like you are just not able to express your feelings well enough to share them with others, at least write them down for yourself, or for other family members to see. I began by keeping a regular journal. It helped me to have a schedule of writing down my thoughts. If you are not used to keeping a journal, just begin by jotting down some notes, anything to get into the habit of writing. If you could get into the habit of writing just one page a week, that would be over 50 pages each year. Don't let the fact that you weren't paying attention to grammar rules during English class deter you. You can edit the results later, or have someone do it for you. As for now, just concentrate on the central point of the story. You might begin by relating how you met your wife, your earliest memories of special holidays, or your favorite vacation. For now, just let the story take its own shape. Another technique that jolts my memory is to look at some old photos. You might be surprised at what surfaces when you are traveling down memory lane. Fortunately for me, my wife and my mother have both been faithful recorders of our family gatherings.

Try not to make it seem like work. If you approach it as something fun, it might help decrease some of the initial anxiety you might be feeling. Just let it turn into something on its own. To think you have to write some great opus when you haven't even written a short story can short circuit the process before you ever get started. There are countless examples of people who discover they have an artistic talent, much to their surprise. And even if the finished product never wows the world, keep in mind why you are writing it. Primarily it's for you, to help make sense of what you're going through, and secondly, so that your loved ones will have an intimate memory of you that they might not otherwise have. If you are the type of person who does not write well, you might also consider the option of telling your story in short snippets into a tape recorder, or have someone you can talk to take notes on your conversation.

Telling Your Story

You'll be surprised how it will help you, and who knows, one day your family members might even thank you. Even if you don't think it's helping right away, it might later on, and even if it doesn't help you, it might help a family member after you're gone. Don't deprive them of that gift. One of the ways I dealt with my initial resistance I had to telling my story was to wonder what it would be like if I had something written or oral from my grandmother. She left a great legacy as it was, but what if I had a little more? I just asked myself what I would give if I could have a book of her stories, a book about advice she wanted to pass down to her children and grandchildren. Well, it would be hard for me to put a monetary figure on it. In many ways it would be priceless. Even though I might think no one would be interested in hearing my story, the reality is that one day someone who might not even be born yet might get some value out of what I share today, a portion of the larger legacy I have left.

Broyard, A. (1992). *Intoxicated By My Illness.* New York: Ballantine Books.

Telling Your Story

It's All In How You Study It...

Chapters

I once read that our lives are like books. They are made up not of days and weeks and years, but of chapters, just like a book. Some of the chapters in our lives are very short; some are very long. Each chapter is a separate unit, and yet, each chapter is also part of the whole story. You can't leave a chapter out of a book or change it without losing the meaning of the story.

I really like this idea. I like to think of the chapters in the book of my own life, and there are a lot of chapters now, with titles like: *Getting Married, Having Children, What It's Like To Have Disabled Children, What It's Like To Go Back To College at 35, Finding God's Purpose For My Life, Losing Children,* and *Preparing To Die.* And the

Telling Your Story

older I get, the more I like the book idea, especially as I get to the final chapter of my life.

Much of my adult life centers around my relationship with Christ and seeking His will for my life. I received Christ as my Lord and Savior at the start of my senior year in high school. Shortly after that time, I began to sense the fact that Christ was calling me to work full-time in a church vocation. The church I was attending was so small that our staff consisted of a pastor and a part-time music director. As this was my only association with church ministry, and I could not sing, I settled on the choice that God was calling me to be a pastor.

Soon after I left home to attend William Carey College, I found out that this was not to be my area of service. I was devastated to realize I was not going to fulfill this call. I was still a young Christian and unable to see that God could still want me to serve him in an area of ministry that I was unaware of. I was so discouraged and began to think that maybe I was unworthy of being used by

Telling Your Story

God in full-time service. I returned home after one year unsure of where I stood in relation to my call to serve God.

I was still unaware of the many ways in which God could use people for ministry, and I married my wife, Lee Anne, and resigned myself to the fact that I could still serve God as a layman. I began work in the golf business and soon afterward our daughter April was born. Six years later, our twin daughters Jennifer and Jessica were born, and everything seemed fine. We were active in church and I was happy in my job. As the twins were approaching their first birthday, my wife and I began to notice they were not progressing as quickly as we thought they should. We were to find out they were severely mentally retarded, even though there were no outward signs to indicate this; they appeared totally healthy. How could something so right go so wrong?

For the next ten years I was completely unconcerned with God and the church. To put it mildly, I was not happy with God and felt we did not deserve this burden. Not only that, I was determined to hide my emotions and not show others the pain I was going through. But slowly I began to work through my feelings and God began to talk to me again about what He wanted me to do with my life. Since my early college days, I had become aware of the many other vocations in the church, especially in the areas of recreation and youth work; however, I was hesitant to even think about the possibility of pursuing such a career because I was 35 years old with basically no college education, and happy with my job. In my wisdom, I could not see how this was going to work. As God began to deal with me, I decided to go to college in the spring of 1987 knowing there were at least four hard years ahead of me. I had told God that the responsibility was on Him because I knew I could not do it on my own.

Through God's help, I was able to finish my college degree while still continuing to work full time. I received my undergraduate degree in 1989 and my master's degree in therapeutic recreation in 1991. I was able to begin doctoral work at Clemson University and for two years worked on projects dealing with accessibility issues for disabled people and sports, specifically golf and fishing. I was on staff at two churches over the next few years and was eventually led to begin working full-time in the health care field working with clients with Alzheimer's, and again I began to settle in to serving God as a layman.

Our daughters were severely disabled and lived quite a long time considering their disabilities. Jessica lived to just short of 18 and Jennifer just over 21. They were the light of our world and the love of our lives. Lee Anne and I were blessed to have them. They were instrumental in teaching us many life lessons: patience, faith, and most importantly unconditional love. While there is something unnatural about children dying before their parents, there was nothing unnatural about the relationship we enjoyed with them, and without them we would have so much less than we have now.

In early 1998, I began another chapter in my life when I was diagnosed with lymphoma. I thought it was the final chapter, but it turned out not to be. I became a cancer survivor. It was a rare type of cancer with the first appearance of flu-like symptoms and an egg-shaped lump

Telling Your Story

on the right side of my neck. My energy level decreased dramatically and I was referred to a specialist. When the diagnosis came, my thoughts immediately went to two specific topics. The first was the stages of death I had learned in my college Death and Dying class. I couldn't remember all of them but I could remember three: denial, anger, and bargaining. I went through those rather quickly. The second topic was from the Old Testament and involved King Hezekiah. He was a king during the prophet Isaiah's time before the children of Israel were taken into captivity. He became ill and Isaiah told him to, "get his house in order," because he was going to die. Instead he began to pray for healing and reminded God of all the areas he had been faithful in. In one of the few instances in the Bible in which God changed his mind, Hezekiah's prayer was answered and his life was extended for 15 more years. Now I'm not here to tell you that I gave God my "report" of what I had done for Him and He rewarded me for being faithful. Far from it. I never even asked God to heal me. I did however ask Him to let me live for five more years because there were some things I wanted to do, and so far it has been eight years. I was able to go to a great immunologist and he chose the perfect treatment plan. His name is Dr. James Holbert, Jr., M.D., Ph.D., and I am extremely grateful for his caring as well as his great care.

I have been trying to adjust to living with a disability and each year watching as my abilities deteriorate further, but I have rediscovered a wonderful truth. In all things, God's grace is sufficient. It releases in us a power that we didn't know we had and gets us through our trials. Not only do we get through it, but we also learn something that will help us in our life later on. I think it's true that when you've gone through your worst trials, that's when you learn God's greatest lessons. During those times you learn something about God's character, or you get a fresh word from Him that is able to sustain you, and you develop a greater intimacy in your relationship with Him.

As I get closer to the final chapter in my personal book, it is remarkable how much of my life has been spent trying to find God's purpose in that book. In many ways it has been the most important chapter. The other day I was reading the Bible and I was just impressed with the thought

Telling Your Story

that this is God's story. In its basic form, it's a narrative about God. Now there are a lot of other people in the book. Noah is in the book. Abraham is in the book, as well as David, Ruth, Peter, John, Paul, and all of the other people mentioned there. They all had a part in the story, but the story is really about God and the ultimate gift of His love for us, His son Jesus. But the Bible is only a story from the beginning of time until the Bible was published. There is an additional story from that time until now and each of us has a place in that story. No one really knows what heaven will exactly be like because the Bible is largely silent about that, but what if one of the things we do when we get to heaven is read everyone else's book, and what part they had in God's story. Or maybe it will be in video form, up on the screen for everyone to see. Then I thought, "How long is my story going to be?" It might be so short that if you blinked you might miss it. Or would I be embarrassed for anyone to see it?

These are just some of the highlights of my life , but I think they give you some insight on the things that have shaped my life and thinking. Jesus Christ is not simply one

Telling Your Story

element of a balanced life, but the center from which an abundant life grows. We as individuals must decide if we are going to run our own lives or choose a Christ-centered lifestyle. God, the Master Planner, the Master Editor, takes these chapters and puts them together, and makes them into a finished book -- a book that is a complete story which makes complete sense. So here lately I have been thinking about my story and asking God to write His thoughts on the tablet of my heart so that I might have a place in His book.

CHAPTER FOUR

Saying Good-bye

As I mentioned earlier in the book, I believe the fear of dying is almost assuredly universal and probably increases for most people as they get nearer to the point of death. But what are the factors that contribute to this fear? The fear of the process may be worse than the product when it comes to dying. What will I die from? For most people my age, the leading cause of death is heart disease, but the most feared is cancer. We fear pain. Will I die alone, as a burden to someone, or in great pain from some debilitating disease? We fear dying alone. We fear that some machine will be keeping us alive. We want a quality life, not just life. And it should be as we lived, within a network of shared relationships. What will happen to my loved ones I leave behind? What's in store for me in the afterlife?

Mental health and pain issues aside, most people are reluctant to die because there is a sense of unfairness about it. I believe it seems foreign and unnatural to us because we have been wired by God to want to live forever. In fact if you believe in a continued life after death in either heaven or hell, we do live forever. No matter how strong our faith, there is a struggle to accept death, and I think this is true whether we are dealing with the death of a loved one or our own death. Because it goes against our nature, most people are reluctant to talk, or even think about, dying. We will even talk about sex, money, or politics before we discuss death, but if denial was an effective coping tool I would choose it as well. Embracing death can have a profound effect on how you feel about your life. In many ways, it can be liberating, especially if you've clarified it in your heart.

If a person is facing a painful death, one topic that often has to be dealt with early on is the choice between aggressive medical treatment and the hospice approach that focuses more on enhancing the quality of remaining life. This decision is ultimately a combination of a person's values, history, personality, sense of community, self-image, and spiritual beliefs, blended together with their medical condition and available treatment approaches. When the pain worsens, you will have to choose between relief from the pain and having a clear mind, because in some cases the only answer is a powerful drug that might affect your ability to realize your surroundings. I have included a more detailed discussion on hospice and other end of life issues in Chapter Seven.

One of the important things I was confronted with when I thought I was going to die was making peace with myself, and more specifically realizing there were things in my life that I was not proud of. There were people I needed to apologize to, and people I needed to forgive. Everyone has what they perceive as unjust things happen to them. It's an inevitable part of life. One of the differences I see in people as they age has to do with successfully dealing with forgiveness. Are they going to choose to hold

Saying Good-bye

a grudge, and the pain that accompanies it, or are they going to forgive and move on with their life? People who can't forgive, or say they can forgive but can't forget, often allow bitterness to take root in their life and ultimately poison it, and the longer they allow that bitterness to remain, the deeper the resentment and pain grows. Many people think, *You don't know what that person did to me. They hurt me too much. I can't forgive them.* I understand the hurt is deep, but I would remind you to consider who the forgiveness is for. The forgiveness may be given to another person but it is ultimately for your own benefit, not theirs. If you knew how seldom the person you're holding a grudge against even gave you a thought, you would not give them that much power over your life. Don't give them the power to continue hurting you by hanging on to the bitterness. Forgiveness is a choice, a liberating one.

A resource I found that really helped me is a book by Dr. Ira Byock, M. D. It is called, *The Four Things That Matter Most: A Book About Living.* It is not primarily a book restricted to people who are facing the possibility of dying, even though he is a palliative care doctor. I'm sure

Saying Good-bye

when he wrote it that he intended it to be more of a daily guide for practical living, and it is that. If a person took the ideals in the book to heart, I'm sure it would improve their everyday life and strengthen their most powerful resources, their relationships with other people. It specifically helped me as I was preparing to die. It is centered around the premise that everyone on certain occasions in their life, but especially as they near death, have relationships that need emotional healing. He says we need to say these four phrases: "Please forgive me," "I forgive you," "Thank you," and "I love you." He recounts stories of the healing power of these words, how they restored relationships that were once considered beyond repair. Even in my life which did not contain that many broken relationships, there were some I needed to restore because I had been hanging on to an old grudge or I had perceived a wrong that had not been intended. There were also some where the relationship was just being taken for granted. I just assumed, like many of us do, that everyone who was important to me knew that I loved them and I knew they loved me, but it never hurts to make those sentiments known. In my case where I've lived eight years past the time I thought I had, it has only made those relationships stronger and more rewarding. Being able to practice saying good-bye as if it were literally the last time I would say it has changed the way I view relationships. It has even changed the way I look at saying good-bye in my everyday language. We say it to each other all the time as a reflex, without ever giving it a second thought that one day that last time you told someone good-bye will be the final time.

I live my life differently than I did before my illness. I try not to leave anything unsaid, especially in my most important relationships. I have seen people at funerals who are trying to talk to a loved one, to ask them for forgiveness for something they either did or didn't say or do, to tell them they wish things could have been different, or to ask them about something they wished they had asked them before they died. These things need to be addressed before someone dies rather than having to try and work through them afterwards.

I have not discussed many spiritual issues in this book, but that does not mean they are not important. They

Saying Good-bye

are sometimes the most important area of your life depending on your cultural and religious beliefs. I know they are in mine, and that's why I focused my thoughts in the story at the end of this chapter on the life that follows this one. I urge you to consider closely the question it poses. In my opinion, it's the most important question you will ever answer. I have noticed in my seminars and discussions with other people that the primary topics centered around financial issues, legal instruments, practical suggestions, and possible resources, so that has always been the primary focus of this book and the website. These issues transcend cultural and religious beliefs.

Byock, Ira, M. D. (2004). *The Four Things That Matter Most: A Book About Living.* New York: Free Press.

It's All In How You Study It...

Going Somewhere

Your culture has a lot to do with your values and beliefs, and this is especially true when it comes to your spiritual beliefs. Most people would acknowledge that they have a spiritual component to their life, but I think that realization becomes stronger as they age, especially as they begin to contemplate their own death. Throughout history, man knows himself to be a sentient being (that is to say: possessing spirit, soul, and body) and that after death we either wind up in heaven or hell. This life is not all there is. In fact, it is only a small part of your life when living forever is factored in. I expect that most Americans believe that there is some form of life after death and that heaven and hell exist, but I know that is true in the South. Very early on, I was exposed to the fact that every living thing eventually dies and you better be preparing for where you will spend eternity, because you're going somewhere. Most people believe that they are going to heaven, and I don't recall meeting anyone who would admit they are going to hell, but I also remember my grandmother saying, "Everybody talking about heaven ain't going there."

If you believe hell is the type of place that I've always heard about, you wouldn't want to end up there. I've never heard it described using any good characteristics. The best I've ever heard it described is as an eternal separation from God. The worst is a place where you experience actual torment and suffering. Heaven, on the other hand, is described in terms of rest, reward, and an eternal relationship with God in a way we have never been able to experience before.

The sticking point begins when you start trying to figure out what is going to determine your eligibility to enter into heaven. This is where culture, values, beliefs, and religion come in. Some people believe that God is a loving God, and eventually everyone will find their way into heaven, because there are a lot of different religions,

Saying Good-bye

and therefore must be a lot of different ways to get there. But I believe that the only factor that will be considered will be your relationship to God, and more specifically with His son, Jesus Christ. As a Christian, I believe my salvation is founded in Jesus, and if you have this same relationship, then you don't have to fear death. Therein lies true peace of heart, for Jesus gives you back the song you were born with, that part of your heart that has been wired for experiencing God. The peace that knowing Jesus provides is that when you die you are saved from the penalty of death and sin and will live with Jesus forever in heaven. There is the security in knowing that nothing you have ever thought, nothing you have ever said, and nothing you could ever do can separate you from the love of God because of your relationship with His son, Jesus. Jesus took all of the anger out of God's voice. When God looks at you now, He only sees Jesus, so that whenever He speaks to you, He only speaks to you in love.

I have held a lot of different jobs in my life. A few years ago, at the request of my wife and mother, I sat down and listed them. There were some places I worked at more

Saying Good-bye

than once, but to my surprise there were 28 of them. Now some people would say that there was simply a lack of commitment, but I was always interested in learning new things, doing new things, and being around people. Probably my favorite job was teaching. I simply loved teaching, and learning, and going to school. Over the years, I have met a lot of people who didn't enjoy school, and I think it's primarily because of tests. Well, at the end of life there is going to be a very important test, and it's only going to involve one question with two parts. The question is going to be, "What did you do with what I gave you?" The first part is going to deal with what you did with Jesus. God sent His son to be the sacrifice for every single person, and He's available to everyone. Your individual sins (past, present, or future) will not send you to hell because Jesus was the payment for those. The only thing that will send you to hell is if you reject Jesus, the payment for your sins. The answer to the first part of the question will determine where you go after your time here on earth, to heaven or hell. I mentioned there was a second part of the question. It's also, "What did you do with what I gave you?" However this time it's referring to your

Saying Good-bye

stewardship of the resources God gave you, not Jesus, but: time, talents, money, and all the other things He has provided for you. How you answer this part of the question will determine your rewards in heaven, but there are no rewards if you don't get in. God has given you the question ahead of time. Make sure you answer it correctly.

Helping_____Die

CHAPTER FIVE

Helping To Put Things In Order

Many people my age are not interested yet in actually preparing to die themselves. However they might be dealing with an elderly parent or parents who are facing their last days, and they would like to know some things that would make this last stage of life go easier. In fact for many people, the reason that someone recommended this book to them is that they are facing this dilemma, which has become known in some circles as the *Boomer Trifecta*. Many people are dealing with at least two, and sometimes all three, of the following financial burdens: saving for their children's education, planning for retirement, or dealing with elder health care issues. I can't really help you with either of the first two, but I can hopefully provide you with some information that can help you with the last one. There are some basic financial instruments that you need to have in place as your loved one prepares for their health care issues or death, such as a will, advance directives, and maybe some type of trust if the estate is large enough to consider avoiding probate taxes. These are all discussed in Chapter Two in greater length.

Additionally, if you are employed and taking care of an elderly parent, you might be able to take advantage of the Family and Medical Leave Act. You should at least know if you qualify for it, and what its provisions are. The first qualifier is determined by the size of the company. If it employs 50 people or more, you are covered by it, and it guarantees you up to 12 weeks a year of unpaid leave - with job security and benefits - to care for an immediate family member with a serious health condition. If you are employed by a smaller company that is not covered by this act, you still might be able to secure a more flexible work schedule, especially if you can convince them of your value to the company. It still costs more to hire and train a new employee than retain a valuable one. You might be able to secure a flex-time schedule, telecommuting from home, and I've even heard of companies, especially those who utilize team building strategies, offering leave sharing, where employees can donate their leave time to fellow employees who need it. At any rate, be proactive. Come up with your own proposal and show them how it can work. You never know if they will consider it if you don't ask.

I left a blank section for the name so you could personalize it to fit your need, but for most people the name that will go in there is Mom.

Helping To Put Things In Order

This is what I see much of the time, and in dealing with the topics for this section I will address the loved one as Mom, rather than leaving the name blank or addressing them as the loved one. She is usually the last one living, and there usually hasn't been much planning on how to pay for those eventual expenses dealing with long term health care. I think many people have just thought that the government is going to help with these expenses, but the reality for most people, unless they die quickly, is that there are going to be some rather large expenses to pay for health care, with no real plan, or help, on how to pay for them. Many of the people I deal with have a plan. It's just not a good plan. Putting it off and avoiding talking about the problem are not good plans.

The best plan is to have long term care insurance, a policy that will pay for expenses associated with long term health care. One of the best aspects of a good long term care insurance policy is that it can help Mom stay in her home as long as possible. It will pay for nursing and custodial care in the home in most instances, but for most people this will not be an option. Mom has waited too late to purchase it, most likely because she never wanted to go into one of those places anyway. Going into a nursing home has a negative implication to most people. They know that most people never return from a nursing home. For the most part, they are there until they die. It may be only a short time, or it may be years, starting first in an assisted care facility, and progressing to a skilled care nursing facility, or even specialized care facility for those dealing with dementia.

Helping To Put Things In Order

If Mom is a widow of a veteran, or if Dad is still alive and was a veteran, there are veteran's benefits available for which they might qualify. I have provided some information on veteran's benefits in Chapter Two, and many geriatric care managers or assisted living administrators are familiar with this program and can help you see if you can qualify for them. However in most cases, the government is not going to be there to help you with long term care expenses, unless Mom qualifies for Medicaid.

Therefore if you don't have long term care insurance, and you've come to the realization that the government is not going to pay for your care, what's the next best alternative? Well, it depends on the resources available. In cases where the husband is still alive, the primary responsibility falls to him. If the husband is no longer alive, or can't provide care, but there are siblings, they get together and develop a plan where they share the expenses to put Mom in a nursing home. If they don't have those resources, they move her from home to home, each keeping her as long as they are able. Often though, the primary responsibility of care falls to one family member, usually a daughter, with other family members contributing financial resources to the extent they are able. One of the things I often hear from people is, "No loved one of mine is ever going into a nursing home as long as I'm alive," or, "I will take care of my wife at home as long as I can." This mostly comes from men and I always want to ask them, "But what if you die first?" or more likely, "What if caring for her kills you?" What then? There may have been a plan in place at one time but things just didn't turn out the way they were supposed to. The stark reality is that unless someone gives a significant part of their life in caring for their loved one, a nursing home is the only choice, and they are very expensive. This is the point where it might be wise to consult a geriatric care manager. I have included a short description of what they may be able to provide for you.

GERIATRIC CARE MANAGER

Some people who are faced with having to deal with long-term care arrangements might well be served to contact a geriatric care manager. They have training in gerontology, social work, or counseling and can usually offer advice in a broad area of services. They have extensive knowledge about the range and cost of services in their area. Geriatric care managers can:

- Identify which services are needed and potential areas where financial assistance might be available, such as veterans benefits.

- Arrange in-home services.

- Assist with the move from home to a retirement community or nursing home. Refer to geriatric specialists where specific interventions are needed.

- Review financial or legal issues and offer money management and guardianship services, especially when dealing with family members who live out of town.

The advantages of dealing with a geriatric care manager may be great when the person responsible for making the decisions for long-term care doesn't really know what the first step should be, or if they live out of town, or if they simply don't have the time or expertise to deal with these matters. You're dealing with one person, so communication is easier and often there is less stress. Services are personalized to the client so the quality of care is enhanced and costs are controlled. As stated in other areas of this book, planning ahead is one of the keys. If you wait until you have to have the services, the decisions may end up being made for you.

One of the things I tell many people, and I will readily share with you that many people disagree with me on this point, is that most people over the age of 70 should not have a house in their name, unless they have some type of long term health care insurance, have enough readily available resources to pay for their health care, or have established some type of trust to protect their estate. Now I admit I'm not an accountant or a lawyer, but allow me to explain why I say this. Most of the people I deal with do not have long term care insurance or enough cash reserve to pay for three to four years of nursing home care. Much of their estate is in their home, and if they were faced with the reality of coming up with the money to pay for extended care at a nursing home, they would have to get it from their house. I have seen this result in a rushed sale of the house, taking out a reverse mortgage, or selling some other asset in order to come up with the money, and sometimes it results in a bad decision. This is especially true if the loved one can't really make a good decision because they have dementia. Then the burden falls to a child having to make these choices, and with our increasingly mobile society, they may not even live in the area any longer.

Now I'm not advocating throwing everyone over the age of 70 out of their houses. This could be devastating, especially to people who have lived in that house for most of their adult life. I'm simply stating that the house should not be in their name. They can still live in a house, even their own house if they're still comfortable living there, but they need to explore options for getting it out of their name. For one, they need to have access to that money in case they need nursing home care, and they will in most cases make a better business decision if they plan ahead and are not forced to sell the house quickly because of time constraints. One option might be to sell the house to someone they trust with the right to rent and live there as long as they would like, but there are many options, and for this decision most people will need to consult a lawyer or accountant.

Helping To Put Things In Order

It's All In How You Study It...

An Old Fashioned Day At Shady Grove

The Browning Family reunion is held annually on the fourth Sunday in April and this year I decided to go a day early and spend some time with my Uncle Vern. We played golf and after spending the night with him and my Uncle Charlie who came down from Corinth, we went to church the next morning at Shady Grove before going to the reunion. It was great and it really brought back a lot of memories. It's been a long time since we all sang at Shady Grove.

It was "Old Fashioned Day" at church and many of the men in attendance wore overalls and the women had "old-timey" hats and what they used to call "swarp-tail" dresses. Now in my mind, the church had not changed much over the last forty years, but in reality it had. Gone were the rows of pews on each side of the pulpit that I used to call the "Amen Corner," which is still clear in my mind, the men on one side and the women on the other. And there's air conditioning now, whereas in my mind every one had a fan. It's been a long time since we all sang at Shady Grove.

But even if some things change, some stay the same. Back then they had Sunday School every week but only had preaching once a month, but they always met together before Sunday School where they sang a few songs and prayed. Well, that's something they still do the old fashioned way, or at least this Sunday. They made a few announcements and sang a song, all the verses (the old fashioned way, if they are going to sing one they are going to sing them all, not just the first and fourth), and had prayer before breaking out to the individual classes. They were studying in Ezekiel in the chapter where it talks about "standing in the gap," and I was able to go in the class where my Uncle Vern was teaching and heard him talk about standing up for what's right and how when you stand up for what's right, you're on God's side because He's on the side of what's right. It's been a long time since we all sang at Shady Grove.

Well, then I went to the reunion and had some really great food and saw a lot of people, some I only see once a year, and I thought of the ones who were here in years past, but had gone on since then. I heard my Uncle Graden remind us that we should remember this time and make an effort to be here every year because there might come a time when we would wish we had. And I heard my Uncle Charlie thank God for being born in the Browning family and how his mom and dad, Odell and Sallie, had done their best as they lived their lives to leave a name we could be proud of, and how it was our job to continue to make it a name to be proud of to pass on to future generations. It's been a long time since we all sang at Shady Grove.

As I got ready to leave, I decided to drive back through the country a little before heading back home. I drove by the old home place and in my mind remembered some of the good times of many years ago. I can still see Miss Sallie feeding the chickens and going to the garden in her sun bonnet, and brushing her hair on the front porch before getting ready for bed. I can still see Mr. Odell going to the barn to milk the cows or feed the hogs and sometimes getting to go with him and even getting to ride the tractor with him. I can still see Uncle Charlie coming up the front steps and touching the underside of the porch roof a couple of times. I can still see those football games out in the pasture with my uncles and cousins, and I still remember the time my Uncle Travis blocked a field goal with his face. As I went down the road and saw an old house about to fall down and remembered places where the houses had disappeared altogether, I thought about how the houses might be gone but the people who lived there would always be there in my mind. Then I found myself back at Shady Grove, not just in my mind but in reality. I got out and listened to the cemetery a little while and thought about how funny it is that I don't like to go to funerals but I actually like cemeteries. As I stood

Helping To Put Things In Order

next to the church, I just closed my eyes and drifted back to earlier times. As I thought back across the years, I could hear voices pleasing to the ear and could see Mr. Odell and Miss Sallie holding their hymnbooks high and Mr. Kirk leading hymns we all used to know. I could hear someone shout "Amen," and it did my soul good. And as I stood there thinking about how I've got more miles behind than to go, I thought it's been a long time since we all sang at Shady Grove.

When I came up on Saturday it probably took about an hour, but it seemed like it took about 40 years for me to make it back home.

CHAPTER SIX

Giving Voice To Their Story

Our parents and grandparents lived lives so different from ours that it is often hard for us to relate to them or understand what they are feeling. We begin this process of understanding by listening to their stories. Often they don't feel their story is important, but it's our job to encourage them, to give voice to their story. Their story is important, regardless of what they may think or say. Try telling your story without their story. It's impossible. You don't exist without them.

If you are having trouble getting them to recall and tell their story, try enlisting other people to help you. There is usually an initial resistance. *Who wants to listen to my story?* Or, *I have a story, but there are just not many things in it I'm proud of.* It will take some encouragement and sometimes you may have to recruit other people to help you in beginning this process. People will do things for a grandchild that they might not do for anyone else. When the request comes from the right person, the resistance will fade.

Giving Voice To Their Story

Have discussion starters for each time you are going to help them with their story. You'll be surprised how easily the stories will flow if you just prime the pump. Ask them about various topics. What are some of the things you are most proud of? What was your biggest regret? What spiritual beliefs were important to you? What was school like? If you knew that you only had a few months to live, what are the things that you would do first? Old photos are an excellent source for discussion starters. I try to let the discussion take its own direction. I don't have a certain idea of how it should go, especially if they bring up the topic. Even if it is only in their subconscious, there is a reason for wanting to talk about it if they bring it up. Another point I try to remember is to never ask why. In getting them to discuss something, I will ask who, what, where, and when questions, but never why. This is especially true if there is dementia involved. Almost everyone will remember certain important events from their particular generation. What were you doing when you first heard about the bombing of Pearl Harbor? Where were you when you heard President Kennedy had been shot? Do you remember watching the funerals of President Kennedy, his brother Robert, or Dr. Martin Luther King, Jr.?

There are a number of resources available to use when encouraging people to tell their life story. One I use is *A Guide For Recalling and Telling Your Life Story*. It was developed for the Hospice Foundation of

America by Dr. Martha Pelaez and Paul Rothman, and the information is included at the end of this chapter. I came across it a few years ago and it is arranged in such a way that it makes it easy for some people to get started. It suggests topics and questions for you to consider under the five main areas of: family, growing up, adult life, growing older, and reflections. Another popular resource is *Families Writing* by Peter Stillman. It provides an easy guide for record keeping and spontaneous writing. There are also "personal historians" available in many areas of the country. They are able to create a type of "ethical will" where instead of creating a legal document to leave your financial assets, you pass along your values as well. In it might be your beliefs, things that you have learned in life, as well as some things you hope for the loved ones you leave behind. They will, for a fee, gather the story and format it into an array of cherished legacies. These range from audiotapes, to videos, to bound books. Two websites you can visit are:

< www.personalhistorians.org >

< www.yourethicalwill.com >

Pelaez, Martha, Ph.D., and Rothman, Paul (2001). *A Guide For Recalling and Telling Your Life Story*. Hospice Foundation of America.

Stillman, Peter R., (1998). *Families Writing (2nd Edition)*. Boynton Cook.

It's All In How You Study It...

Being A Browning

What's in a name? A lot more than just letters. It's a legacy. But a legacy of what? One of my favorite things to do is to make sure that I go to as many family reunions and Christmas functions as I can. I especially like the Browning "get-togethers." One I remember vividly happened a few years ago when my Uncle Charlie talked about how thankful he was to have been born into the Browning family. And even though my last name is not Browning, I knew I was a part of it as well.

Well it got me to thinking about what kind of legacy I was passing on to my future generations. The Bible talks about the curses of iniquity visiting the children for three or four generations, and it also talks about God keeping a covenant of mercy lasting for a thousand generations. What kind of legacy am I leaving? The decisions I make are going to have consequences for generations to come. No person lives or dies to themselves. I like to think about it like an account at the bank. What is in my account? Am I leaving blessings of mercy or curses of iniquity? And if I'm trying to leave blessings, what does my account balance look like?

I remember Charlie talking about how that even though they didn't have a lot of money, they never considered themselves to be poor because they were rich in love. He remembered his mother and father teaching him and his sister and brothers that it was just as easy to say something good about somebody as it was to say something bad. That you didn't tear somebody down in order to feel better about yourself. That is was just as easy to overlook a wrong as it was to hold a grudge.

I realize that my life is better due to my ancestors. Even when things are not going as well as I would like, I know they could be worse if it were not for the ones who went before me. I know that many of the good things I have experienced were because of the seeds of faithfulness my grandparents had planted. They were storing up blessings in their account that have been passed down to me and hopefully continue to be passed down to future generations. They especially did this through prayer and being givers. They were praying people and generous givers. They were praying people because they knew that prayer changes things and that God would honor their faithfulness through their children and grandchildren. They were generous givers even though they weren't wealthy. Giving has little to do with wealth. Giving is an attitude. Stingy people will find a way to be stingy and generous people will find a way to be generous in spite of their money. My grandparents would find a way to do it with compliments and smiles even when the money was not there. They did it through forgiving someone who had wronged them. They did

Giving Voice To Their Story

by going to church even though they were tired. And they did it every time they gave up something they really wanted so that their children or someone around them might have something they wanted. They were storing up blessings. A Godly heritage is better than great wealth.

I mentioned earlier that hopefully these blessings would continue to flow down to future generations. This will only happen if I play my part. First, I have to make sure that I'm living in such a way that I don't block those blessings. If I am only concerned about what I need and what I want to do, then I will not only block those blessings from flowing down to future generations, but I can leave curses of iniquity, a legacy that they have to spend much of their time overcoming. Second, I have to make sure that I'm adding to those blessings. It's one thing for me to want better things for myself, but it's another thing entirely for me to want to have God bless my children and grandchildren. Am I making sure my mercy account is full? I know how to do it. I've had the best role models a person could ask for. I am a Browning.

CHAPTER SEVEN

Dealing With Hard Decisions

This chapter contains some difficult topics for discussion, specifically dealing with how to deal with Alzheimer's and other types of dementia, hospice care, and other end of life issues. I have touched on some of these issues in earlier chapters, but I have waited to cover them more fully in this section because I have usually had to address these issues when dealing with people who were trying to help someone else die.

DEALING WITH DEMENTIA

Have you ever thought which would be worse, to have a good mind and the body goes, or to have a good body and the mind goes? For most people, it's the latter, especially as they age. When you talk to people in general about the type of death they fear most, it's usually the

Big C - cancer. However if you talk to older people, it usually centers around dementia, and more specifically Alzheimer's disease, because people seem to lose the very characteristics that make them who and what they are - human beings. But Alzheimer's is only a subset of the larger dementia disorder, somewhere between 50 - 60%. There are categories of dementia other than Alzheimer's disease, but the very word Alzheimer's conjures up fear. It begins with a gradual loss of memory, and then progresses quickly to impact every area of your life, as well as the lives of everyone providing care for you. Much of the conflict usually centers around the appropriate level of care, and how best to transition to that level and deal with the conflicts that arise.

Dementias are usually divided into three broad categories: neurological based, general medical disorder based, and primary dementias. The first category includes Parkinson's disease and damage from strokes. These conditions can sometimes be slowed if they can be diagnosed early and treated properly, but if allowed to progress, functional ability and personality can be severely altered. The second category contains dementias that can be traced to a general medical disorder, such as AIDS, syphilis, and thyroid deficiencies. The third category, primary dementias, are usually incurable and irreversible. The most prevalent one in the last category is Alzheimer's disease, but also includes alcohol dementia syndrome and other rare disorders such as Pick's disease. There have been studies in the last few years trying to determine the effectiveness of drugs in slowing the progress of Alzheimer's disease, but trials have yielded mixed results. Aricept and other drugs have worked for some patients, but usually the effectiveness is defined in terms of slowing progression, and seldom in reversing symptoms. As the symptoms worsen and the patient loses more functional ability in areas of memory, judgement, and emotional stability, they usually become more of a burden on their caregivers and may eventually end up in nursing home care.

LACK OF SOCIAL SUPPORT

One of the things I've noticed about people who are most at ease with the dying process is that they have a good nucleus of support people around them. I bet if I had looked at their life 20 years ago they still would have maintained a group of people around them who shared their values, supported their interests, and wanted them to be successful. Friendships are an important base for any successful person. But as we age, life begins to be about losses, and how we deal with them. No one consciously says *I'm going to isolate myself*, but it often ends up that way. As our friends die, we don't replace them, because we get too busy or too tired, and before we know it, we've pretty much decided to go it alone. Then things start to gain a momentum on their own, and the cycle of depression, helplessness, and isolation takes on a life of its own. If your loved one still has a good social support system, then you have some valuable people available to help you. Sadly, most of the cases I encounter have very little in the way of social support resources to assist them.

From a social and emotional standpoint, it's hard to imagine any death worse than to die alone and unloved, to feel isolated and that your life has been meaningless. In many of these instances it's because the individual has pushed everyone away and lived their last years as if they needed no one, but sometimes I have seen people feel this isolation while surrounded by loving friends and family. These friends and family members may try to offer help and support, but the individual has trouble receiving it because of their own internal feelings of unworthiness. Perhaps they have guilt over something they did or didn't do, or have self-doubts of their worth, and often they refuse offers of help based on these feelings.

A few years ago, there was a story in our local paper that emphasized this very scenario. A man was found in his house, having died almost a week earlier. He wasn't found by a family member or friend coming to check up on him, but instead by someone in the neighborhood who heard the crying of the cats. When the police came, they found the man, but also found over 50 cats. And over the next few days, this became the focus of the story, the cats. How could a man have all of these cats in his house and none of the neighbors even notice? How could he live in all of the filth found inside the house? And, most importantly, what was going to become of these cats? Almost nothing was ever said about the man. How could he have fallen through the cracks of society, dying alone with no visible social support system? Within days, there were two groups that deal with cat rescues willing to take in and place all the cats in good homes, but there was never a follow-up story on the man and how this could have happened. All of the remaining stories focused instead on the cats and their well-being.

Maintaining friendships becomes even more important as we age, especially for men. I say especially for men, because men are often the ones who feel that they can be the lone wolf, and don't need other people. When you get to the point that you can count your friends on one hand, that ought to be a warning signal. And I don't just mean acquaintances, but real friends. In our society, we've almost forgot what it means, and takes, to be a friend. Friends do things together. They stay in contact with each other, even if it's just to touch base. Like they used to say when I was growing up friends would ask, "How's your mama and them?" We knew what that meant. What's been going on? How is your family? Friends celebrate with each other, and grieve with each other when it comes time to grieve. There's an old saying that a friend can halve your sorrow and double your joy. Friends hold each other accountable. They tell each other when they're getting off course. Friends stand by you even when you've done something wrong. But friendship takes work, or it will dissipate. If you want a friend, you have to be a friend. Maintaining a friendship is not as hard as beginning one, but it still takes work and a willingness to spend some time and energy on the relationship.

WHERE DO YOU WANT TO DIE

This may sound like an odd question at first, but I see families struggle with this quite often. I must caution you at the outset to think about this question before giving your loved one the option of choosing where they die. If you know you can't care for them at home, even with hospice and other resources available to you, then don't offer them that choice. If you know that it's going to be too painful for you to remain in the house after they die there, then be honest about your feelings. My father-in-law recently died and my wife and her siblings were able to offer enough assistance to their mother so that he was able to die at home. This was what he wanted but it was a lot of work on everyone's part, even with hospice care. I had two children die at home, and for my wife and I, this was the best option. In our case, it was the best decision we could have made. I personally can't think of a more depressing place to die than a hospital. I was glad both our daughters were able to die at home, in comfortable and familiar surroundings, surrounded by people who knew and loved them. Our case was different than other cases in that the care they received at home was as good as they could have received at a hospital. They were both in the end stages of respiratory failure and we were able to have oxygen and nursing care, so for us it was the best situation. I also must tell you that there was a financial aspect to the decision. Their quality of life at the end would have been no better at the hospital, and the only difference was the cost and the logistical burden of one of us having to be at the hospital 24 hours a day to make sure we were there when they died.

At the risk of sounding like I'm on a soapbox, our society still hasn't figured out how to deal with end of life issues because our hospitals are full of people who don't have much of a future from a quality of life standpoint. One of the things I hope this book accomplishes is to increase the frank discussion of some of these end of life issues so that people can make wise choices. I have often talked to people who wished they could have helped their loved one die at home. They just didn't know how to make it happen or that there were options available to them. With hospice it is much easier for a person to die at home if that is their wish, and if they have to die in a nursing home or hospital, hospice services are also available there.

If you choose to let your loved one die at home, you should strongly consider hospice care. This sounds like a simple choice to let some one with expertise in end of life issues help you with some of the decisions you might face. But for some people hospice is not an option they will consider, or they might wait until the last minute to consider it. If you don't have hospice and your loved one is going to die at home, you should talk to your physician about Physician Orders for Scope of Treatment (POST). This is a physician's order sheet that is often used when a patient is being transferred from one facility to another, but can also be useful if a patient wishes to die at home. If a patient has decided what treatment procedures they want at their end of life and has discussed them fully with their physician, then they can complete this document that specifically states what treatment they wish to receive. POST documents normally carry sections dealing with cardiopulmonary resuscitation (resuscitate CPR or DNR), comfort measures for pain, medically administered fluids and nutrition, and antibiotics for treating new medical conditions. Some of these decisions may already be addressed in a living will or health care advance directive, but the POST orders can be helpful in dealing with the do not resuscitate decision if an ambulance is called. Most paramedics or emergency medical technicians will attempt CPR if they are called to the house whether the patient or the family wishes it, unless there are POST orders. There are a few things you need to be aware of with POST orders. They must be signed by a physician to be valid. Any incomplete section of the document implies full treatment, so care must be taken to make sure they are properly completed in order to assure that the patient's wishes are honored.

HOSPICE

Hospice is one of those words that evokes a great deal of emotion in people, most of it negative. For many it signifies the end, giving up. For that reason, I usually talk about hospice in terms of the services provided, rather than using the word hospice. It is not abandonment, but instead a shift in medical priorities. For terms of definition, it is usually defined as specialized care for people in life's final moments. It emphasizes dignity, comfort, and pain management, and seeks to address the patient's social, emotional, spiritual, and physical well-being, as well as their family members. As a professional treatment modality, hospice is still in it's infancy in America, only about 30 years old, but it is becoming increasingly accepted as Americans continue to age. There are two categories of hospice companies, profit and non-profit, but there are few differences when it comes to services provided. Companies are usually reimbursed on a daily fee basis which is not based on their organizational structure. Hospice care is usually delivered at home, but can also be provided in a hospital, nursing home, or assisted living facility, or at another family member's home.

The typical treatment team includes the patient's attending physician and the following hospice team members:

    Medical Director
    Registered Nurse
    Social Worker
    Certified Nursing Assistant
    Chaplain, and
    Volunteers

Hospice typically provides medicines, medical supplies, and equipment related to the illness, as well as professional nursing services. The primary reimbursing sources of payment for these services are Medicare, Medicaid, and private insurance, but patients are accepted for hospice based on need, not the ability to pay, so most hospice organizations will work with the family in dealing with payment options.

Hospice care is usually instituted with the diagnosis of a terminal illness and a physician's referral and prognosis that the patient has six months or less to live. Many end stage illnesses qualify for hospice care, but the most prominent ones include: cancer, congestive heart failure, ALS, HIV, AIDS, COPD, renal failure, liver disease, end stage stroke, and Alzheimer's and related dementias including Parkinson's. I mention Alzheimer's specifically because many people don't think about

Alzheimer's qualifying until the very end days, but if you have a good physician who is adept at identifying stages you can usually qualify in stage five and six, with seven being the end stage. This brings up an important point. Most people don't consider hospice care early enough, and when they do, it's usually because the physician brings it up. They think that if they discuss the topic it is admitting defeat, so instead it's easier for them to remain in denial. I seldom see anyone who felt they received hospice services too early, but I hear all the time about those who waited until the last few weeks before accepting help, often wishing they had done it earlier. You don't have to wait for the doctor to bring up the topic. Be proactive. The earlier a patient accepts hospice services, the more the patient and family members benefit. And it doesn't have to mean the end of hope. The word hope is contained within the seven letter word hospice.

WHAT DO YOU WANT YOUR FUNERAL TO LOOK LIKE

Lastly, you need to talk about what your loved one wants the actual funeral to look like. Many people say, "I don't care what happens at my funeral because I won't be there," but I believe you need to talk about specific items, who will officiate the service, what music will be played, and even down to what clothes you want to be buried in. The more plans you have in place will make the process go more smoothly for your family and friends left behind. They may already be in grieving, so take a little time beforehand to plan some aspects of the funeral so they won't have to make those decisions. Having to guess at what you would like to happen can add stress to an already difficult situation.

Hopefully some advance planning has taken place with the burial plot and casket already having been selected, and maybe even most of the arrangements having already been paid for. Any reputable funeral home can help you with these advance planning decisions. But for many families, especially in cases of unexpected death, these decisions are just added to the list of many others that have to be made. And sometimes when decisions have to be made in stressful situations they are not always the best ones, especially when dealing with the cost of the funeral. In this book I can only talk of financial costs in broad terms because they vary widely throughout the country, but funeral expenses can easily reach the $5,000 - $6,000 range, especially if you choose the traditional method of the burial plot, casket, and other funeral home related expenses.

Cremation has become an alternative to many people over the last 35 years. In 1970, almost everyone still chose the traditional method, but in 2005 almost 30% of people chose cremation, and industry sources estimate than in the next 25 years that number could reach 50%. Much of the reason for this growth is financial. The average cremation costs as much as one third less than a traditional funeral. But there are other factors, many cultural and spiritual, to consider in making this decision. I know that for my mother and father cremation would not be an option, and I think this holds true for many people born in the South. The area where I live, Tennessee and Mississippi, has the lowest percentage of cremations, less than 10% in 2005, while the largest percentage of cremations occur in the western states and Hawaii, over 60%. I know the overriding factor for my mother and father, and many others in the South, is spiritual. For other people, where the body is located after they die is not the most important factor. Again, communication is the key. Discuss these issues with your loved ones and make some plans beforehand. For me, these decisions are best made when times are good rather than during a crisis.

It's All In How You Study It...

The Good Old Days

I've always heard people talk about the *good old days*, and I have a couple of questions. What made them the *good old days*, and when did they end? For me, part of the *good old days* has to do with a sense of freedom and independence when there weren't a lot of responsibilities yet. Growing up, my world was as far as I could walk or ride my bike, as long as if it didn't require riding on a major thoroughfare. Most of my life took place within the boundaries of my elementary school, the playground where summers were spent playing box hockey and tetherball, Rakestraw's store where I bought penny candy that really cost a penny and those Coca-Colas in the small size bottles which were just the right size to hold a bag of salted peanuts after you took a couple of swigs. There was the Whistle Stop/Sno Cream Castle where I picked up my papers for delivery on my afternoon paper route, and the drug store where I bought my "had to have" new comic book issues.

There were summers filled with baseball games, bikes with baseball trading cards in the spokes, hula-hoops, making clover necklaces, and lying in the grass on your back and picking out cloud shapes. You played 45's and LP's on a Hi-Fi, and there were still restaurants with jukeboxes at the table. Melanie sang, "I've got a brand new pair of roller skates, you've got a brand new key." Today you would have to explain what a roller skate key is.

I heard my parents talk about party lines and even I remember when telephone numbers had a word prefix to identify the exchange. Mine growing up was FAirfax 7-2346. I also remember GLendale, WHitehall, and BRunswick. I remember my grandparent's refrigerator with the glass door inside the metal door, so that you didn't have to let all the cold air out if you just wanted eggs, mustard, or catsup. And in the top, there were no side by side's then, was a metal ice cube tray with a release lever to eject the ice.

The TV had to warm up. I had a 1956 Chevy where the gas went in the taillight and you could take the key out of the ignition and the car would still run. And speaking of cars, service stations were still full service. You got trading stamps when you bought gas, you got your windshield cleaned with a smile, and the air was free. If you would have told the attendant that one day air would cost money, he would have thought you were crazy. And wasn't it great when they would have gas wars, with 29 cent gas? And McDonald's were 15 cents and Krystal's were three for a quarter.

Dealing With Hard Decisions

And when did the *good old days* end? It makes sense that if they're not the *good old days* anymore, there must have been a day when they ended. Often people have certain events that stand out in their mind as "red letter" days and most people can tell you where they were and what they were doing on that day. It's different for each generation: Armistice Day, the day Pearl Harbor was bombed, the day President Kennedy was assassinated, the explosion of the Challenger space shuttle, the end of the Berlin Wall, 9/11, and many others.

I talked to one couple who said that while these days might not be as good as they have been in the past, they are still good because their spouse is still here to enjoy it with them. While left unsaid, I got the impression that the death of their spouse would be **That Day** that changed everything forever. After then, the *good old days* would be few and far between. For everyone there's going to be a **That Day,** the day that's going to change everything. For many, it will be a death of a spouse or a close family member. But until then, enjoy the *good old days*.

Appendix

Appendix

GLOSSARY

ADVANCE DIRECTIVES - Advance Directives are end-of-life documents in the event you become unable to speak for yourself. The two most popular are the living will and the health care power of attorney.

CPR - cardiopulmonary resuscitation.

DNR - Do not resuscitate.

HEALTH CARE POA - This is sometimes referred to as a Health Care Power of Attorney or a Medical Power of Attorney, or a Durable Power of Attorney for Health Care. This document authorizes someone to act on your behalf as your attorney-in-fact in making your medical decisions, after it has been determined that you can no longer act in this capacity. Your health care power of attorney does not have to be a lawyer. In fact, most of the time, it is someone very close to you who you trust to carry out your previously expressed decisions.

HOSPICE - Specialized care for people in life's final moments. It emphasizes dignity, comfort, and pain management, and seeks to address the patient's social, emotional, spiritual, and physical well-being, as well as their family members.

Appendix

INTESTATE - Dying without a will.

LIVING WILL - A living will is a legal document that says you don't wish to be hooked up to any life support systems that artificially prolong life in the event you are terminally ill or permanently unconscious and unable to communicate.

LTC INSURANCE - Long-term care insurance provides money for when you need care for activities you can no longer provide for yourself, and for supervised care if you develop dementia. In-home care and adult day care can be covered by it, and assisted-living facilities and nursing homes accept it.

POST Orders (Physician Orders for Scope of Treatment) - This is a physician's order sheet that is often used when a patient is being transferred from one facility to another, but can also be useful if a patient wishes to die at home. If a patient has decided what treatment procedures they want at their end of life and has discussed them fully with their physician, then they can complete this document that specifically states what treatment they wish to receive. POST documents normally carry sections dealing with cardiopulmonary resuscitation (resuscitate CPR or DNR).

Appendix

PROBATE - At a person's death, any assets in their sole name are frozen and are subject to the probate process, even if there is a will. One of the reasons for probate is so that any creditors can file a claim with the person's estate, and the state and federal government are the first in line. The negative aspects most of us associate with probate center around the issues of time, cost, and the fact that the proceedings become part of the public record.

REVOCABLE LIVING TRUST - This is a document that gives you control over your estate at your death or in the event you become disabled. It allows you to leave your assets to whom you want, when you want, how you want, and in the most tax efficient manner. Many people who have a living trust do so in order to avoid probate. It is usually drawn up by an attorney, but you can create one yourself if you're comfortable with the legal process.

Appendix

Long-Term Care Questions

How much will long-term care cost?

Skilled nursing home costs can be very expensive. In our local area, it approaches $50,000 per year, and in other states that figure can be almost twice as much. In-home care is less unless you are talking about round-the-clock home care.

What are the chances that you will need long-term care?

Nationally, about 40% of those over 65 need long-term care. This year, that amounts to about seven million people. By 2008, that is predicted to rise to over ten million. Currently, over 75% are cared for at home by family and friends.

If you have to go to a nursing home or assisted-living facility, what is the average length of stay?

According to Health and Human Services, the average length of stay in a nursing home is two-and-one-half years. About 10% of those residents remain for more than five years. In an assisted-living facility, the average is about 18 months.

Appendix

Who pays for long-term care?

According to the Health Care Financing Administration (HCFA), about 40% of costs are paid by Medicaid, but only after you have spent down your resources to the poverty level. About 18% are paid by Medicare. The rest, nearly one-third, are paid by individuals and their families out of their own pocket.

How do LTC insurance policies work?

The insurance company charges you a premium based on your age and health situation. You are buying a pool of funds which is available to you to spend on your long-term needs in the future should you need care. You will purchase a daily benefit for a specific period of time. The daily benefit will be for assisted-living or nursing home care. Additionally there will be a lower daily benefit to cover in-home care and adult day care centers.

What about inflation?

Most companies offer an inflation protection option that will increase your daily maximum benefit over time to help keep up with inflation.

Appendix

What payment options are available?

Companies offer a variety of options, from single-premium, annually, 10-year pay, to age 65, and life.

Do you have to keep paying premiums if you start receiving long-term care?

Your policy should have a waiver of premium in the event you require covered care, but you should make sure that it waives the premium for all types of care, not just if you go into a facility.

What about deductibles?

Long-term care insurance companies call their deductibles elimination periods. Based on how long you think you can pay for the cost of care out of your own pocket, you choose an elimination period, such as 30, 60, or 90 days. The longer elimination period you choose, the lower your premium, and sometimes this may be 20% or more lower. You only have to meet this elimination period one time.

Appendix

Can you deduct the cost of LTC insurance from your income taxes?

Most polices are tax-qualified, but you need to make sure. Then you will be able to deduct the cost of the policy from your income taxes, provided you meet the 7.5% minimum on Schedule A, form 1040. You need to consult with your tax preparer for a final determination of whether you can deduct these costs.

Do you have to pay income taxes on the benefits received from a LTC policy?

No, not as long as the policy is tax-qualified.

Who determines when benefits are paid?

Your doctor must certify that you have met the requirements of the policy and prescribe a plan of care. Most policies are triggered in one of two ways: (1) you need substantial assistance with at least two out of six activities of daily living (eating, bathing, dressing, toileting, transferring, and continence), for a period of at least 90 days; or (2) you need substantial custodial care to protect your health and safety due to severe cognitive impairment.

Appendix

How are the benefits paid?

Once you have met your elimination period, your policy will pay for incurred expenses up to the daily benefit. You have to provide copies of the costs and then you will be reimbursed, and most policies will not cover expenses to friends, neighbors, or family members. There are policies that contain an indemnity clause (for an additional premium) that will pay the full daily benefit regardless of actual expenses.

Will your premiums go up if your health deteriorates?

Most policies are guaranteed renewable as long as you continue to pay your premiums. Premiums can only be raised for the entire class, not on an individual basis.

Are Alzheimer's, Parkinson's, and other dementias covered?

Yes, as long as it is diagnosed after the policy is in force.

CPSIA information can be obtained at www.ICGtesting.com
Printed in the USA
LVOW051929170513

334355LV00001B/196/A